10/1

Artwork by Christina Kent

THEY DRAW & COOK ™

Artwork by Alexander G. Savakis

Artwork by Sarah Straub

Nate Padavick & Salli Swindell present:

THEY DRAW & COOK ™

107 Recipes Illustrated by Artists from Around the World

weldon**owen**

COOKING IS SUPPOSEd TO bE fUN, RIgHT?!

YuMmy yUm YuM!

We think recipes should be fun too . . . and encourage people of all ages to be creative in the kitchen.

WHAT'S NOT TO LOVE about cute kittens cooking, funny monsters munching, 16-handed chefs and smiling watermelons?! So, in February 2010 we started a blog called They Draw & Cook as a place for anyone with a passion for art and cooking to show and share their love of both by bringing their favorite recipes to life through illustration. We've received hundreds and hundreds of amazing recipes from artists all over the world and are continually in awe of their talent and creativity.

THIS BOOK CONTAINS a sample of 107 illustrations that range in style from cute to goofy to absolutely gorgeous. They are funny, tell stories, amuse, engage, and delight—and sometimes make you want to reach in to take a bite! Some of the recipes are detailed: let them guide you. Others are open to interpretation: let them inspire you. All of the recipes are beautiful: we know they'll amuse you.

THE ARTISTS whose work you see in this book, and on the website, are a varied and talented bunch. Some of them are professional illustrators and practicing artists, while others are passionate doodlers and drawers, and a few have only recently begun to draw. Please visit their websites and blogs (listed at the end of this book) to encourage them all to continue adding beauty to the world. We wish we could have included every single recipe posted on theydrawandcook.com (there are hundreds!) in this book because they are all terrific and deserve to be seen by everyone. When you're ready for more more more, please visit our website, theydrawandcook.com, to see the entire collection.

WE WANT TO THANK all the artists who joined in the fun and helped turn They Draw & Cook into a treasure trove of inspiration. A big thanks also goes out to Roger Shaw, Hannah Rahill, and Emma Boys at Weldon Owen Publishing, and our agent, Kitty Cowles, who understood from day one how fun it is to draw and cook!

WE HOPE THIS BOOK inspires you to cook up something new or maybe even pick up a pencil and doodle out your own favorite recipe and play along by visiting our website:
theydrawandcook.com

ENJOY!!
Nate Padavick
& Salli Swindell

Gust's Scrambled Eggs

(and egg cracking technique)

Last meal I made for Gust before he left this world.

To crack eggs. swing the sharp edge of a butter knife into an egg...

butter knife ✗ swing

...for a clean break.

(According to Gust cracking an egg with a butterknife nearly eliminates the chance of shells falling into the egg white. No one wants crunchy scrambled eggs.)

← Sharp edge

1 T. milk

2. Before whipping eggs with a fork or whisk add a tablespoon of whole milk. (Gust says the milk smooths out the eggs. water dilutes the texture.)

3. Melt butter (not oil, Gust says) in a frying pan.

4. When butter starts to bubble add egg mixture.

Gust recommends cooking eggs until just firm (NOT HARD!)

Add salt and pepper to taste. Enjoy!

Eliza's Somewhat Famous Veggie Quiche

1 9-inch refrigerated piecrust

5 eggs

1/2 cup cherry tomatoes (chopped)

2 cups chopped spinach

1 bunch green onions (chopped)

1/2 cup sliced portabella mushrooms

3 pressed cloves of fresh garlic

2 tablespoons olive oil

1/4 cup real mayonaise

1 cup gruyère cheese, grated

1/2 cup double gloucester cheddar cheese, grated

1 pinch of rosemary (fresh is bestest!)

1 pinch thyme

salt & pepper to taste

dash of nutmeg

Preheat oven to 375°F. Fit the crust into a 9-inch pie/quiche plate.

Heat olive oil in a skillet over medium-low heat. Add the green onions, garlic, and portabellas & sauté for 5 to 7 minutes.

In a large bowl, whisk together eggs, mayonaise, rosemary, thyme, nutmeg & salt and pepper to taste. Stir in the onion mixture, other veggies, the gruyère & cheddar.

Pour the egg mixture into the crust. Bake until a knife inserted in the center comes out clean, 40 to 60 minutes. Serve & enjoy :)

eliza devogel 2010 :)

if you think you've had

Egg
(wel

♡

you will need...

Eggs 2 –Beaten

Tomatoes ↓ –chopped

① fry Egg + ⅓ garlic till just cooked.

② remove Egg + fry Tomato, ⅔ garlic

KETCHUP

Red Sauce

3 minced garlic cloves

Salt + oil.

10 oz
Bacon
Chopped

1 1/4 cups
Heavy
Cream

1 cup
Milk

Pastry

1/3 lb
French
Emmental
Grated

put,
beat,
add,
bake,
300°F (150°C) - 30 min

serve.

Bon appétit !

Lorraine

(leu kich lowen in english) Preparation time : 20 min

BACON & EGG TOASTIE...

It's A Bit of a cheeky cure for the evil HANGOVER!

STUFF YOU NEED:

- One fresh egg from a happy Chicken.
- Two to Three rashers of bacon from a happy Pig.
- Two slices of toast from a lovely loaf.
- Some tasty Tomato Sauce.
- Oh, and a glug of good oil to fry.

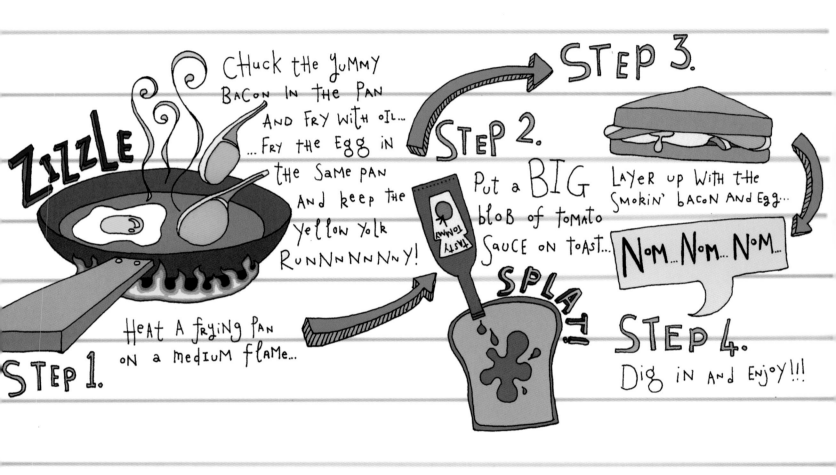

PUT TWO HANDFULS OF DRIED FRUIT IN A SUITABLE RECEPTACLE...

(IF YOU HAVE LITTLE HANDS PERHAPS ADD A BIT EXTRA)

...ADD BOILING WATER (CAREFUL NOW) & LEAVE TO SOAK FOR 10 MINUTES

BUTTER OVER A LOW HEAT (WATCH THAT IT DOESN'T BURN).

TO THE MELTED BUTTER ADD 1/3 CUP OF BROWN SUGAR &

1/2 CUP OF MARMALADE. STIR UNTIL EVERYTHING MELTS.

MELT 2/3 CUP OF UNSALTED

NEXT, SLOWLY, ADD 4 1/2 CUPS OF ROLLED OATS & MIX UNTIL THE OATS ARE COAT

DRAIN THE SOAKING FRUIT...

(IF THE MIX IS TOO DRY SAVE SOME WAT

...& ADD TO THE MIXTURE, ALONG WITH

A HANDFUL OF CHOPPED NUTS (IF YOU WAN

GIVE IT ALL ONE FINAL STIR & POUR INTO A

FOILED SHEET

ADD 2 TBSP. OF HONEY
OR GOLDEN SYRUP
IF YOU PREFER

BAKE
325°F
25 MIN

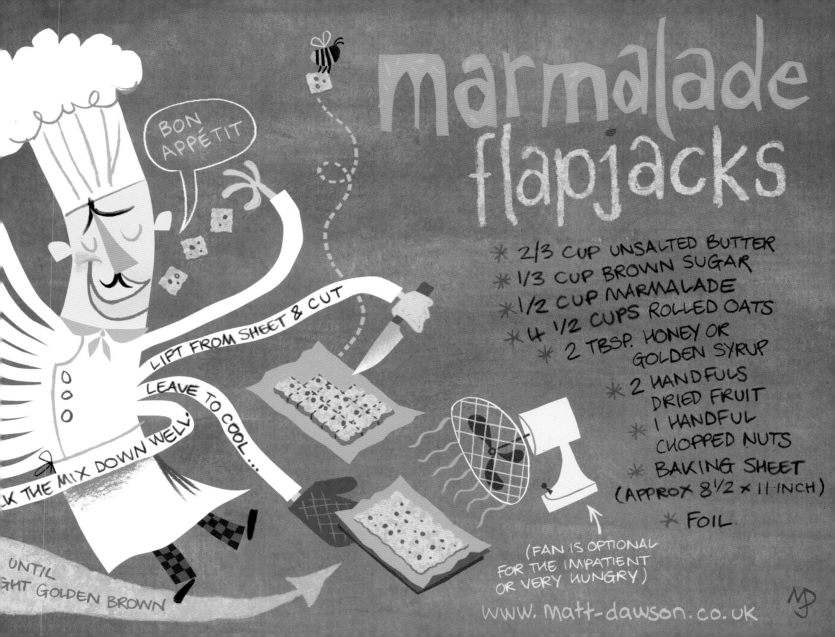

THE BRION FAMILY ~RECIPE~

EASTER BREAD

INGREDIENTS

2 packages dry yeast
1/4 cup warm water
1 cup milk
1/2 cup sugar
1 tsp salt
8 tbsp butter

3 eggs
5 1/2 cups flour
1 1/2 tsp vanilla
grated Lemon rind
Slivered Almonds

DIRECTIONS

1 place 2 eggs in a bowl with warm water

2 Combine yeast with ¼ cup warm water. Let sit.

3 Combine milk, salt & butter. Warm over medium heat until melted. Let Cool.

4 Beat eggs into milk mixture. Stir in vanilla, lemon rind, then yeast.

5 Add 2½ cups flour & beat until smooth. Add rest of flour and mix with a spoon or hands if necessary.

6 Knead dough on flat surface til Smooth. Let dough rest for ten minutes & knead again.

7 Put dough in oiled mixing bowl. Cover with damp Cloth. Let dough rise in warm place for about an hour.

8 Punch down dough. Divide it into 3 long pieces & braid together to make a nest. Wrap braid around an egg and tuck the end underneath.

9 Cover nest with a damp cloth again. Let it rise another 10 minutes.

10 For Decoration, Brush nest with milk, Sprinkle sugar, and pierce bread with Slivered Almonds.

11 Bake in oven at 325°F for around 30 minutes until bread is light gold in color.

enjoy!

Blueberry Bran Muffins

Makes 12 muffins

1 1/4 cups unbleached all–purpose flour
1/2 cup whole wheat flour
2 teaspoons baking soda
1/2 teaspoon table salt

1 large egg
1 large egg yolk

2/3 cup packed light brown sugar
3 tablespoons mild molasses
1 teaspoon vanilla extract

6 tablespoons butter (melted and cooled)

1 3/4 cups plain yogurt

2 1/4 cups bran cereal

1 cup blueberries

1. Adjust oven rack to middle position and heat oven to 400°f

2. Spray muffin pan with nonstick cooking spray

3. Process half of bran cereal until finely ground, about 1 minute

4. Melt butter in microwave, set aside

5.

Whisk flours, baking soda and salt in a large bowl to combine; set aside

6. Whisk egg and yolk together in medium bowl until well–combined and light–colored, about 20 seconds

7. Add sugar, molasses, and vanilla; whisk until mixture is thick, about 30 seconds

8. Add melted butter and whisk to combine

9. Add yogurt and whisk to combine

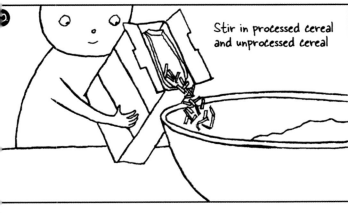

Stir in processed cereal and unprocessed cereal

11. Let mixture sit until cereal is evenly moistened, about 5 minutes

12.

There will be small lumps, that's okay

13. Add wet ingredients to dry and gently mix with rubber spatula until batter is combined and evenly moistened

14.

DO NOT OVER MIX

15. Gently fold blueberries into batter

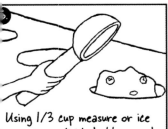

Using 1/3 cup measure or ice cream scoop, divide batter evenly among muffin cups. Do not level or flatten surface mounds

17. Bake until muffins are dark golden and toothpick inserted in center of muffin comes out with a few crumbs attached, 16-20 minutes

18. Cool muffins in pan for 5 minutes

19. Transfer to wire rack and cool for 10 minutes before serving

20.

ENJOY!

rose petal jam

(a fairy favourite recipe)

1. pick petals

b

ingredients

1lb petals

2 2/3 cups sugar

8 cups water

juice of 3 lemons

2. place petals in

add **half** the sugar

& mix together

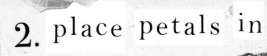

3. leave over night

(sweet dreams)

z z z z z

in

o m

o w l

5. place in jam pots

(yum-yum)

4.

add the lemon juice, water & left over sugar

to a pan. dissolve the sugar by heating the

mixture carefully. stir in the petals and simmer

for 20 minutes. then bring to the boil

until the mixture goes nice & gooey.

© cally johnson-isaacs

Smoked Mackerel Pâté

Chop the
spring onions

Remove the smoked
mackerel's
skin
and bones;
flake the flesh

Mayonnaise

Squeeze the juice
rom half of
lemon
Add
2 tablespoons
of mayonnaise
The best
with fresh,
unchy bread!

Mom's Crab Dip

8 oz. package
of cream cheese,
softened

1 pound can
of lump crabmeat

3 T mayonnaise

3 T (or more)
horseradish

Mix everything together.
Put in a buttered pan.
Cook for 30 minutes at 350°f degrees

7 layer DIP

1. refried beans + hot sauce + med. heat

2. extra virgin olive oil + high heat + scallions + green salsa + cilantro

3. black beans + cumin + med. heat

4. chipotle salsa

5. lime zest and juice

6. 2 avocados + garlic cloves + 1 lemon + 1 jalapeño

Tzatziki
Matteo's mom's recipe

ingredients
cucumber
greek yogurt
salt garlic
mint

1 Salt

2 cucumber on the salt

3 wait an hour, throw away the salt.

4 + + = cut the mint and the garlic

5 mix the cucumbere, the mint, the garlic and the yogurt.

Recipe → Place one sheet of frozen puff pastry on a cookie sheet. Tha[t]

15-20 mins @ 350°F. Cool 10 mins. My mouth is watering.

[s] shown. Place a nicoise olive in the center of each shape. Bake

P i S

a d i

Melt 2T butter + 2T olive oil. In a large pan. Caramelize (4) thinly sliced onions over a very low heat til golden. It takes an hour but it's worth it. (Cool. Spread over pastry. Arrange anchovies in a patte

s a l

è r e

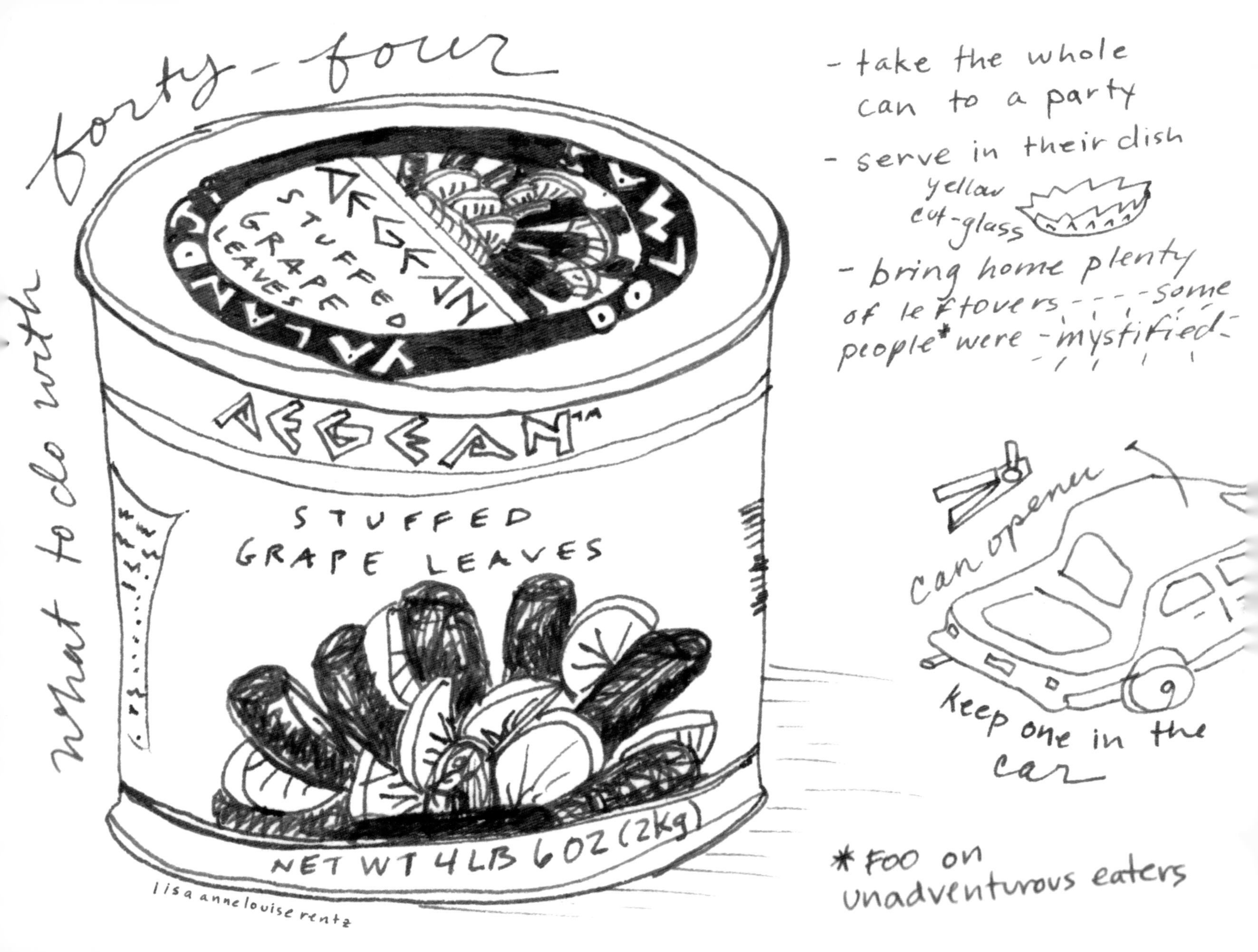

what to do with forty-four
AEGEAN STUFFED GRAPE LEAVES
YALANDJI DOLMA
AEGEAN™
STUFFED GRAPE LEAVES
NET WT 4 LB 6 OZ (2Kg)
- take the whole can to a party
- serve in their dish
yellow cut-glass
- bring home plenty of leftovers ---- some people* were - mystified -
can opener
keep one in the car
* Foo on unadventurous eaters
lisa anne louise rentz

...nese SGLs are lemony, the RICE
...side is juicy + the leaves are
...hewy — both in a goood way.

SERVING suggestions

▷ SGLs are dressy- pair with left-overs!
▷ go with any fresh veg.
▷ blobbo of fat-free yogurt on the side

minty sweet tea

*not cooked? local

SGLeaves simmered in their juices

r snow peas? passed into? hot?

grape leaves

and juicy

salt

big

farmers snow peas

green

serrano

pepper

sweet potato half

*baked with bread — same heat!

salt

FF yogurt

salsa

mini cheddar

sausage

biscuits

fry, don't stir

GOOD HOT -and- COLD

a napkin

enjoy dinner & teevee

and then

you ra ng?

FIORI DI ZUCCA FRITTI

FRIED ZUCCHINI FLOWERS

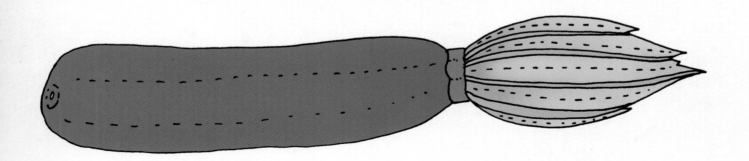

2

eggs
2

flour
1 cup

milk
1/4 cup

beer
3/4 cup

16 blossoms

3

peanut
seed oil

OIL

seasoned with
salt and pepper

Salsa verde:

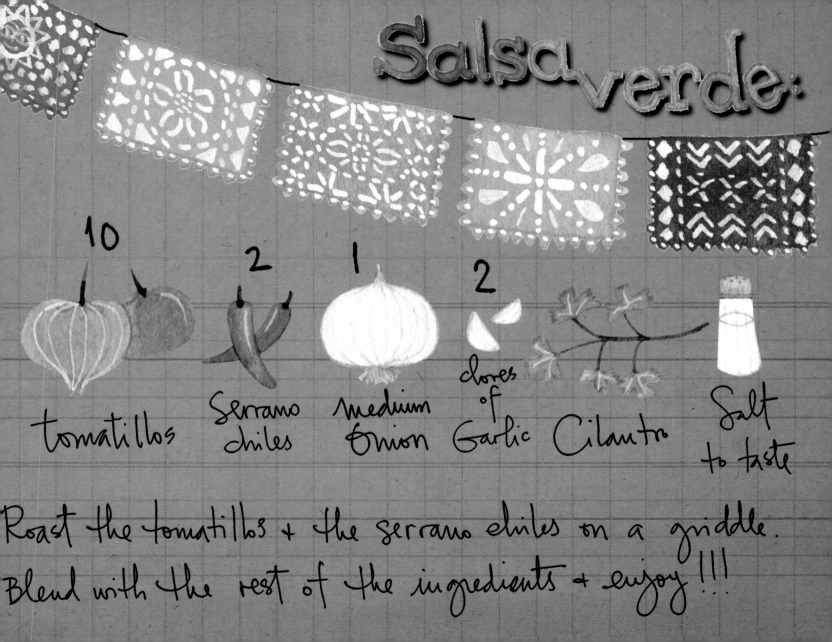

10 tomatillos

2 Serrano chiles

1 medium onion

2 cloves of Garlic

Cilantro

Salt to taste

Roast the tomatillos + the serrano chiles on a griddle. Blend with the rest of the ingredients + enjoy!!!

Arugula

Pink Grapefruit

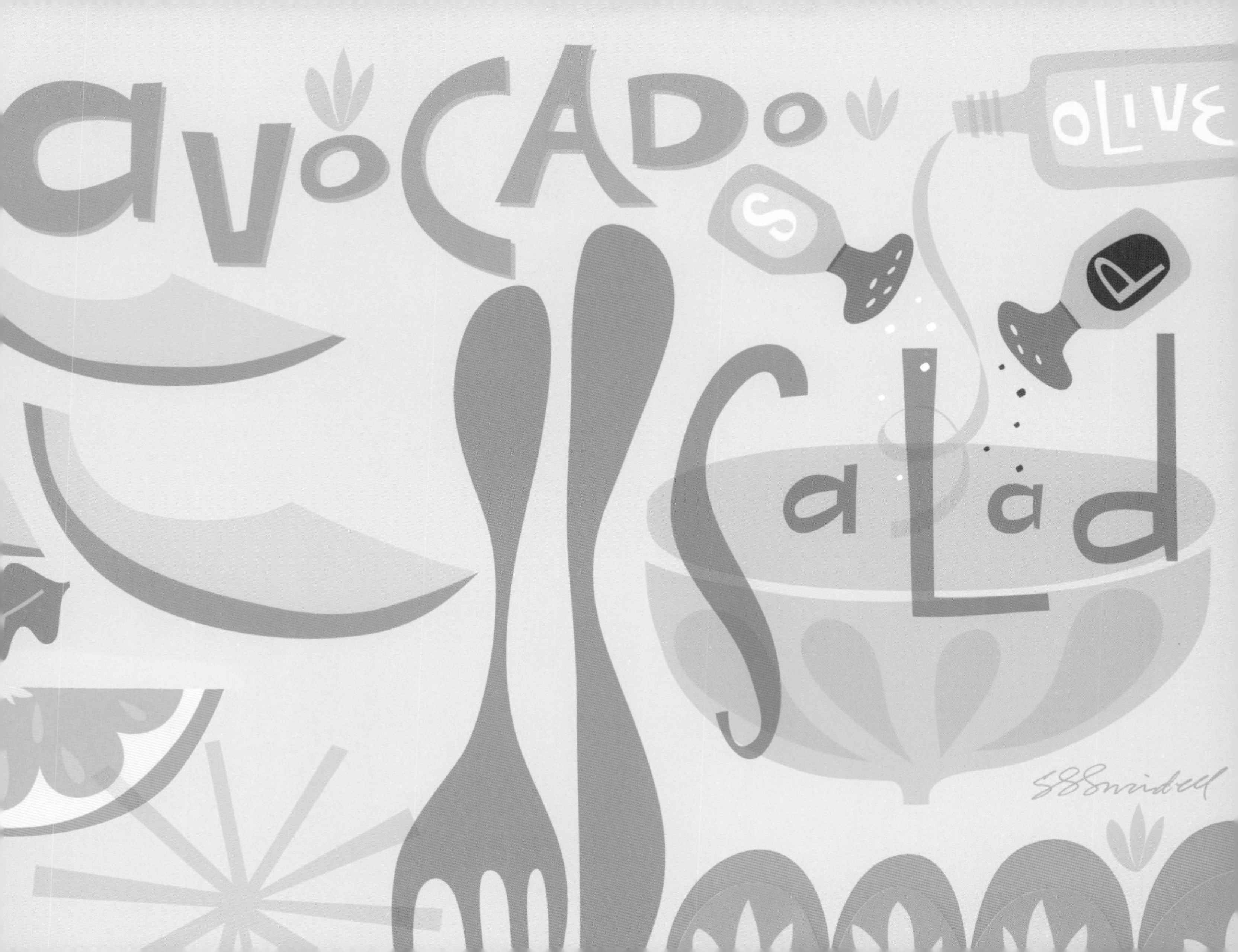

AVOCADO
OLIVE
S
P
Salad
SSSwindell

Georgia
Chicken Peach Salad

1. wait for summer

2. buy peaches in season

3. toast chopped pecans to bring out their wonderful flavor

4. cook chicken with salt, pepper and 1tsp. olive oil

5. cut chicken and peaches into bite size pieces

6. in a large bowl, combine chicken, peaches and lemon juice, mix gently

7. in a smaller bowl, combine the yogurt, green onion and a small squeeze of lemon juice

8. divide the greens among four dinner plates

9. add the chicken and peach mixture, pour dressing on top of the mixture, sprinkle with chopped roasted pecans

Enjoy!

1lb Chicken Breasts

4 Peaches

2tb Lemon j

Salad Greens

S P

RAW BRUSSELS SPROUT + RADish SALAD

1. SHRED SPROUTS
2. CHOP RADISHES
3. MIX IN A BOWL

-WITH-

OLIVE OIL
LEMON JUICE
CASHEWS
+
SALT

GOAT CHEESE BERRY SALAD

1 bag arugula

3 oz. crumbled goat cheese

1/4 cup pine nuts

1 cup cut up strawberries

1/8 cup basalmic vinegar

1/4 cup olive oil

Mix all ingredients together in a bowl.

Toss, serve and enjoy!

Cold BEETroot SOUP

cook it when the weather is hot!

A

Ingredients:

- a big beetroot
- cucumbers } depending
- hard boiled eggs } on number of portions

How to Cook:

Bouillon: boil 8 cups water + grated beetroot. In 5 minutes add salt and lemon juice to your taste. Leave it to cool.

Grate cucumbers & eggs, then add to the soup.

Garnish with spring onions and parsley.

Bon appetit!

Persian Lentil Soup

Add → 2 Cups green lentils,
3 Tablespoons vegetable oil,
2 Large onions peeled and thinly sliced,
4 Cloves garlic peeled and crushed,
Salt/ Pepper/ Turmeric/ Saffron
To → → 5 Cups Of Water →
Bring to a boil → Simmer for 40 + min.

arugula

walnuts

white grapes

lettuce

olive oil

vinegar

salt

parmesan

Top Model Salad

Watermelon soup

Components:

1/2 cup
of condensed milk

3/4 cup
of sour cream

3 1/4 cups
of raspberries

2 pounds
of watermelon

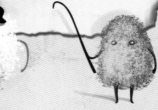

2 teaspoons
of sugar

1 teaspoon
of vanilla sugar

Recipe:

4 - 6 servings

1. *Pick out watermelon seeds. Purée watermelon with raspberries, milk, sour cream, sugar and vanilla sugar.*

2. *Purée well with two cups of water and refrigerate for one half hour.*

3. *Pour soup into bowls and garnish with raspberries.*

Enjoy your meal!

Moroccan Orange

4 Large Oranges,
rind & pith
Removed

icing
sugar

icing
Sugar

12 dates,
stoned &
quartered
Lengthways

½ tsp
ground
cinnamon

3 Tbsp
Rose
Water

Rose
Water

handful
fresh
mint,
Roughly
Chopped

& Date Salad

Arrange oranges on the plate, scatter with the dates, then sprinkle rosewater on top. Scatter with mint, then dust with icing sugar & cinnamon.

A refreshing end to any meal. Enjoy!

@kim.

2-16 oz. cans refried black beans

1-28 oz can crushed tomatoes

1-16 oz box chicken broth

2 cups cooked cubed chicken

Serve with oven-toasted
tortilla strips

& grated Parmesan
cheese

BLACK BEAN & CHICKEN SOUP

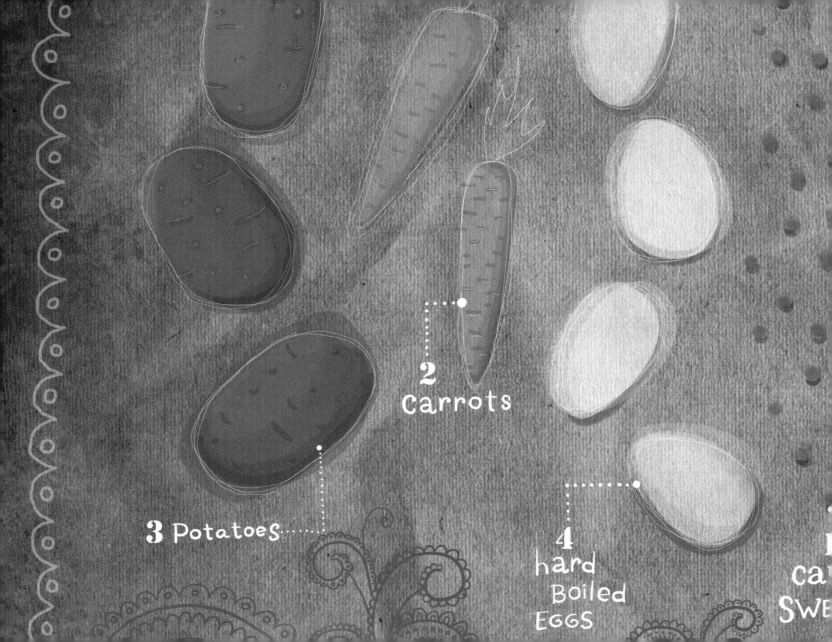

2 carrots

3 Potatoes

4 hard Boiled Eggs

ca
Swe

2
Pickles

1/4 lb.
Salami

1/2
jar
mayo

Salad
Olivier

- boil vegetables and dice
- add pickles, sweet peas and diced salami
- finish with mayo and salt
- ENJOY

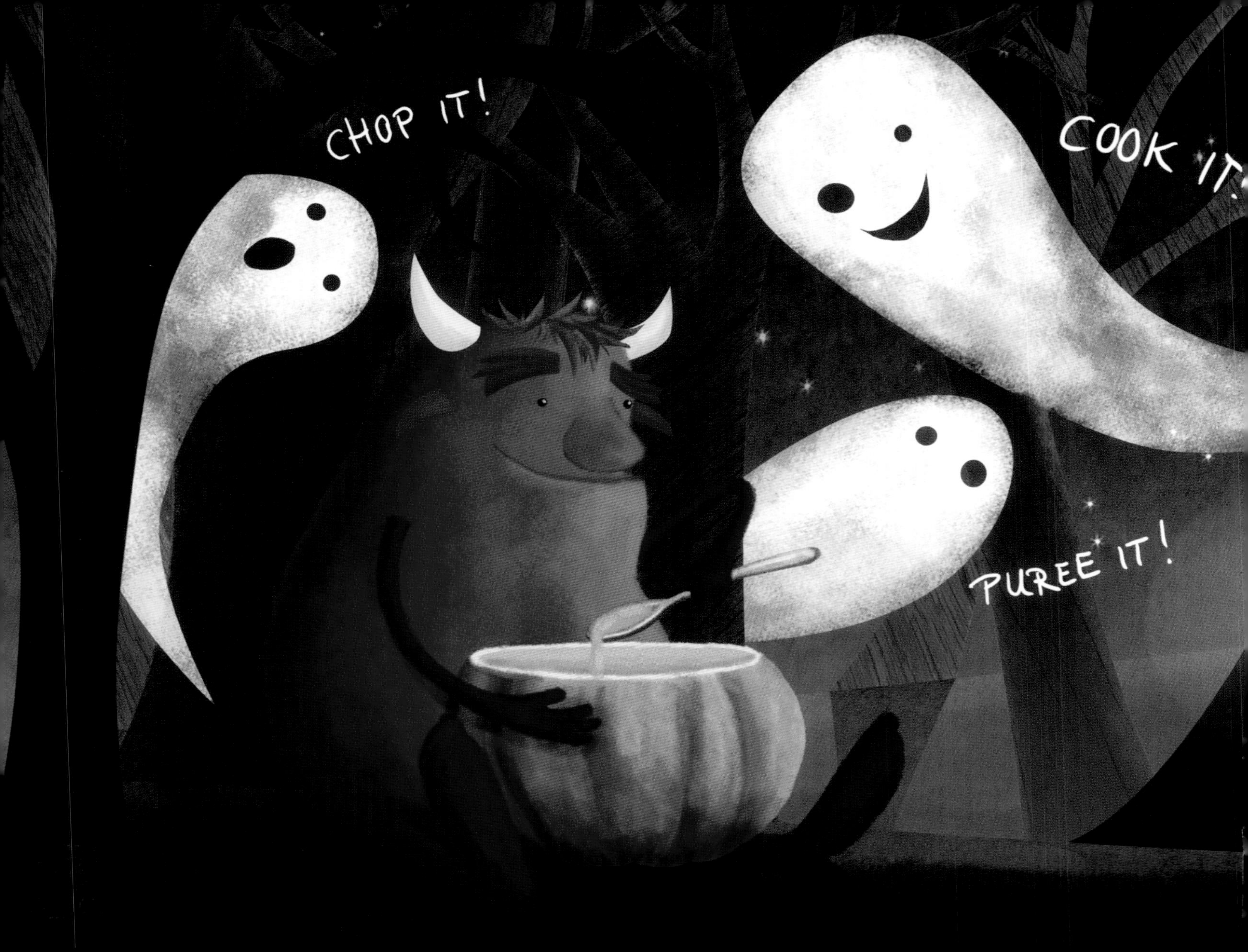
CHOP IT!
COOK IT!
PUREE IT!

MONSTER's *favourite*
PUMPKIN
SOUP

1 cup
Cream

1 Medium - sized
Cooking Pumpkin

2 Cups Vegetable Stock

1 spoon Butter

1 Onion

1 Garlic Clove

1 Orange

Stuffed Portobellos

Ingredients:

S

P

Panko

Tomatoes

4

Portobello Mushrooms

CHOPPED CHIVES

Mozarrella CHEESE (SHREDDED)

Directions:

remove gills from mushrooms

broil for **5** minutes (gill sides down)

Combine other ingredients

stuff mushrooms with mixture

broil them again for **5** minutes

sliced bread

hazelnut &

emmental cheese

CH
SA

Indian Ricotta

PANIR

2 C - diced into 1/2 inch cubes

spinach
10 Cups

Garlic

4 cloves

Ingredients

3/4 cups onion finely chopped

1/2" piece ginger grated

Method
1. Blanch the spinach in boiling water.
2. Drain and blend to a smooth puree.
3. Fry the panir in hot oil till golden. Drain & keep aside.
4. Heat oil, fry the onions till translucent

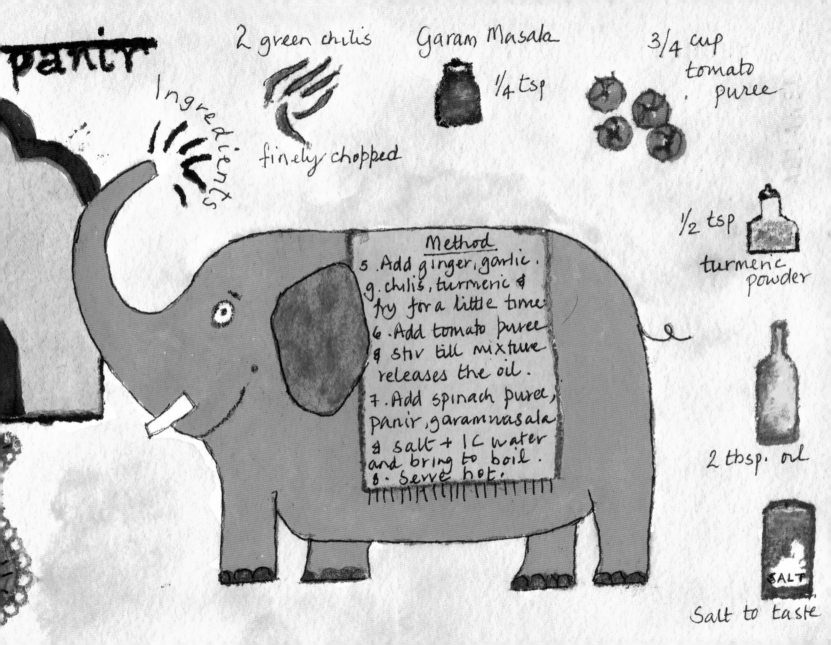

panir

Ingredients

2 green chilis
finely chopped

Garam Masala
1/4 tsp

3/4 cup tomato puree

1/2 tsp turmeric powder

2 tbsp. oil

Salt to taste

SALT

Method
5. Add ginger, garlic,
g. chilis, turmeric &
fry for a little time.
6. Add tomato puree
& stir till mixture
releases the oil.
7. Add spinach puree,
panir, garam masala
& salt + IC water
and bring to boil.
8. Serve hot.

INGREDIENTS
Serves 4
1 1/2 pounds russet potato
1 savoy cabbage finely she
1 leek, pale green parts
cut into 1/2 inch dice.
1 cup soy milk
1/4 teaspoon nutmeg
coarse salt

COLCANNON (fat-free & vegan too)

DIRECTIONS:

1. Peel and boil potatoes until tender, about 15 minutes.
2. While potatoes boil, combine cabbage, soymilk, nutmeg, leeks and salt. Cook over medium heat until cabbage and leek are soft, about 15 minutes. Mash the cooked potatoes and stir in the leek and cabbage.
3. Spread mixture into an eight inch baking dish and place under the broiler for five minutes.

Serve with fake sausage links, peas and sliced tomatoes... a pint of Guiness won't hurt this a bit.

K. Reilly

FIDEUÀ

HELLO GUYS! TODAY WE'LL COOK "FIDEUÀ", IT'S LIKE A PAELLA, BUT INSTEAD OF RICE, IT'S MADE WITH PASTA. WE'LL NEED THESE INGREDIENTS:
SOME FISH BROTH
GROUPER OR MONKFISH
SHRIMPS OR PRAWNS
CUTTLEFISH OR SQUID
MUSSELS OR CLAMS (OPTIONAL)
13 OUNCES THICK NOODLES
OIL
1 / 2 HEAD OF GARLIC
1 LARGE TOMATO
1 TABLESPOON PAPRIKA (SWEET OR SPICY)
SALT

1. FRY THE SHRIMPS OR PRAWNS WITH SOME OIL IN THE PAELLA PAN.

2. FRY ALSO THE MONKFISH GROUPER AND THE MUSSELS CLAMS.

6. ADD THE BROTH WITH THE FISH AND THE SEAFOOD. TASTE IT BEFORE ADDING SALT.

7. THE AMOUNT CAN BE VARIABLE APPROXIMATELY TWO PARTS OF BROTH BY ONE OF NOODLES. STIR ALL THESE INGREDIENTS.

3. USE THIS TO MAKE THE BROTH IN A POT WITH SOME WATER.

4. LET THE BROTH BOIL UP TO HALF AN HOUR QUALITY AND SCENT ARE VERY IMPORTANT.

8. LET IT COOK FOR ABOUT 15 MINUTES. WAIT 5 MINUTES BEFORE SERVING.

5. NOW, MAKE THE "SOFREGIT" SAUCE IN THE PAELLA PAN. START WITH THE GARLIC, THEN ADD TWO SHREDDED TOMATOES AND THE PAPRIKA.

GARLIC TOMATO PAPRIKA

NOODLES

ENJOY THIS AMAZING FIDEUÀ!

12 FRESH
SAGE LEAVES,
TORN

2 DOZEN
BUTTERNUT SQUASH
-OR- PUMPKIN RAVIOLI

1/2 C. TOASTED WALNUTS,
COARSELY CHOPPED

1 STICK BUTTER

1/2 C. DRIED
CRANBERRIES

GROUND
PEPPER

1 SHALLOT,
FINELY CHOPPED

FRESHLY GRATED
NUTMEG

FRESHLY GRATED
PARMESAN CHEESE

butternut SQUASh RAVioli
with CRiSPY Sage brown butter sauce

1. BRing a large pot of WATeR to a boil. MEANWhile, chop shallots
    AND toasted walnuts.

2. GENtly add RAVioli to boiling WATeR AND cook ACCORDINGLY.

3. While pasta is cooking, melt butter in a large skillet over medium
    heat. Add sage, shallots, cranberries AND walnuts
    AND cook until the butter starts to
    brown, about 3-5 minutes. Remove from heat
    AND season with pepper AND nutmeg.

4. GENtly plate RAVioli AND top with
    brown butter sauce. SPRiNkle with
    PARMEsan cheese AND serve.

SERVES 4. PReP time 30 minutes.
Pairs well with pumpkin ale.

Betsy Snyder

Mum's amazing tomato couscous

I always ask my mum to make this, it's so simple and tastes amazing. Great as a side dish at BBQs, it reminds me of summer, but I have it all year round. Great for lunch, and it's vegetarian too.

Serves 4

2 tsp white wine vinegar

You will need:

8 oz couscous

7 oz diced feta cheese

1.25 cups vegetable stock

1 can cherry tomatoes

3 tbsp olive oil

2 red onions

handful basil leaves

salt and black pepper

3 tbsp capers

What to do:

1. Drain the can of tomatoes, keeping the juice as you'll need it in a bit.

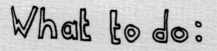

These are getting cooked with the cous-cous.

You'll be making the dressing from that

2. Put the couscous in an ovenproof dish and pour the stock over it. Add the tomatoes (minus the juice) and the basil.

Stir it all together

Cook at 375 °F for 20 minutes.

3. While it's cooking, blend the tomato juice with the vinegar, 1 tbsp of the oil, and some tabasco sauce if you like. Season with salt and pepper.

You can also add a bit of sugar if you're that way inclined.

4. Heat the rest of the oil in a frying pan, and whack your red onions in. Fry until nice and golden then add the feta and capers and cook for a tiny bit more, but don't melt the feta completely.

Guarantee you'll have seconds - yum yum yum.

5. Take the couscous out of the oven, and mix in the red onion concoction. Serve onto plates and drizzle generously with your tomato dressing. Enjoy!

Vegetarian Meatballs

Sauté an onion with garlic, cumin, and coriander.

Combine with 1 cup cooked adzuki beans, 1 cup cooked bulgur wheat, and 1 beaten egg.

Add breadcrumbs until you can roll a firm ball.

Broil for 12-15 minutes.

Enjoy

starving artist goo-lash

(otherwise known as poverty casserole

me, circa 2001

nine lives and 30 lbs ago...

actual size of my apartment, no room for furniture or utensils or guests weighing more than 85 lbs

this recipe was a staple in my very small, but very expensive, apartment in New York.

other ramen noodle.

instructions

$5

1 lb. ground chuck
(the fattier, the cheaper)
mmmm... fat!

1. Cook macaroni til' mushy.
2. Cook meat til' it's brown.
3. Mix all ingredients well.
4. Eat it out of the bowl.

nom, nom, nom

for god's sake, don't buy any known brands! you won't be able to buy that box of wine!

canned* tomatoes
(canned! jars are
way too pricey!)

*remember- dented cans
are even cheaper!

ACME
ELBOW
MACARONI

TOTALLY
GENERIC
TOMATOES

*if that freelance check
comes in- splurge on some
powdered parmesan!

FAUX
PARM

Yummy!

box o' no-name
elbow macaroni

Coupons are
for wussies!
Love, Lisa

keep in the fridge (if you have one) for up to... well, until it smells funny.

spaghetti alla caruso

· onion ·

Here's what you need ~

1 lb. chicken livers
1 cup flour
2 tbsp. olive oil
2 tbsp. butter
2 cloves garlic, chopped
1 onion, chopped
1-2 cups mushrooms, sliced
1 cup dry red wine
1 · 28 oz. can San Marzano tomatoes
1/4 cup parsley, chopped
1 lb. spaghetti
a little salt and pepper
Some parmesan cheese

· chicken livers ·
(kinda yucky raw — yummy cooked)

· butter ·

· cloves of garlic ·

OLIVE OIL
from olives

GOOD WINE
· DRY ·
made from real grapes

Spaghetti

Enrico Caruso was a famous Italian opera singer.
This is a dish he liked to cook for himself.

.enrico caruso.
.famous opera guy.

Here's how to make it ～

Season the flour with salt and pepper.
Dredge the chicken livers in the flour.
Brown the livers in a pan, then set aside.
   (brown them with the olive oil)
Add some butter to the pan, and saute the
   garlic, onions and mushrooms for 5 minutes or so.
      (don't burn them)
Add the wine and reduce down to about half.
Puree the tomatoes and add them to the pan.
Slice the livers in half and add them to the pan.
Season with salt and pepper.
Cook on low heat for about a half an hour.

Cook the spaghetti.
Drain the spaghetti.
Mix the sauce with the spaghetti.
Garnish with parsley and grated cheese.
Serve and eat and enjoy!!

.canned san marzano tomatoes.

CENTO
blah blah blah blah blah
ITALIAN
SAN MARZANO PEELED TOMAT
NET WT. 28 OZ. (1 LB. 12 OZ.)

.real fresh san marzano tomatoes.

.mushrooms.

.flat leaf italian parsley.

.parmesan cheese.

thyme
12 branches
or so

parsley
a couple dozen
branches

sorrel
a handful
or two

basil
a couple
handfuls

a few handfuls
of lovage

or—

greens from one bunch of celery

1/2 an onion, diced and sauteed until tender

a clove or two of garlic, minced

chop

chop the herbs fairly fine, but leave some texture

put the herbs into a bowl with 2-3 tbsp of olive oil and 2-3 tbsp of margarine or butter

mix with ½ cup wheat germ or bread crumbs, toasted, then toss with cooked pasta

pasta
with handfuls of HERBS

ZUCCHINI & SUMMER SQUASH RISOTTO

FOR 3-4 SERVINGS

1 CUP RICE
(SHORT GRAIN OR ARBORIO)

5-6 CUPS BOILING
WATER OR CHICKEN BROTH

1/2 SMALL ONION, CHOPPED
1 GARLIC CLOVE, CHOPPED
1/4 CUP OLIVE OIL

1 ZUCCHINI, GRATED

1 SUMMER SQUASH, GRATED

SALT & PEPPER

2 TBS FRESH BASIL, CHOPPED

1-2 TBS BUTTER

1/2 CUP PARMIGIANO-REGGIANO GRATED + EXTRA FOR TOPPING

1 PUT THE ONION & GARLIC IN A LARGE SAUTE PAN & DRIZZLE WITH OLIVE OIL. COOK OVER LOW HEAT UNTIL ONION IS SOFT.

2 ADD THE RICE & COOK FOR A FEW MINS TO TOAST.

3 MEANWHILE, HEAT UP WATER OR BROTH IN A POT UNTIL SIMMERING. ADD 1/2 CUP AT A TIME TO RICE & STIR OFTEN. ADD MORE BROTH WHEN THE RISOTTO HAS ONLY A LITTLE LIQUID LEFT.

4 AFTER 15 MINS OR SO TASTE THE RICE, IT SHOULD BE AL DENTE (FIRM TO THE TOOTH) THE RISOTTO SHOULD BE A LITTLE SOUPY.

5 ADD VEGGIES, CHEESE & BUTTER. STIR OVER HIGH HEAT TO TIGHTEN UP THE SAUCE.

6 REMOVE FROM THE HEAT, STIR IN THE BASIL & SEASON WITH SALT & PEPPER. LADLE INTO BOWLS & TOP WITH CHEESE.

cook + drain

fry

mix

cream

bake

Swiss Alpine Macaronies

serve with cooked 🍎 slices

DELI

FRESH BASIL

FRESH PARSLEY

P
E

OUS BAS!L PESTO ⇒

⇒

* a great base for sauces
or simply spread on hot toast

AM
AN
EESE

CASHE
—WS

SEA
SALT

blend ingredients with a mortar & pestle

add oil,   a little lemon zest

and garlic to taste

peel and grate potatoes
mix with flour and salt until sticky 'n' doughy
dice and fry pork
make 3 inch balls
fill with fried pork
boil in large pot 50ish. min
enjoy with butter
and lingonberry jam

+ pork + salt = palt

Chicken in Love
Place your favourite chicken parts to bathe in a special mix with these ingredients:
massage the chicken!
salt
yogurt +
ginger
pepper
soysauce
olive oil
garlic
garam masala
minimum: 10mins
ideally for: 2hours

STIR-FRY CHICKEN UNTIL IT TURNS A BIT GOLD.

MIX, MIX, MIX MIX, MIX WELL!

LITTLE HONEY

CAYENNE PEPPER IF YOU LIKE IT HOT

SALT + PEPPER

FINELY CHOPPED PARSLEY + CORIANDER ↳ LOTS OF IT !!!

SERVE WITH THIS MAGICAL SAUCE ⟶

SPRING ONION

GAR LIC

SOY SAUCE

LEMON JUICE

OLIVE OIL

on Appétit ♪

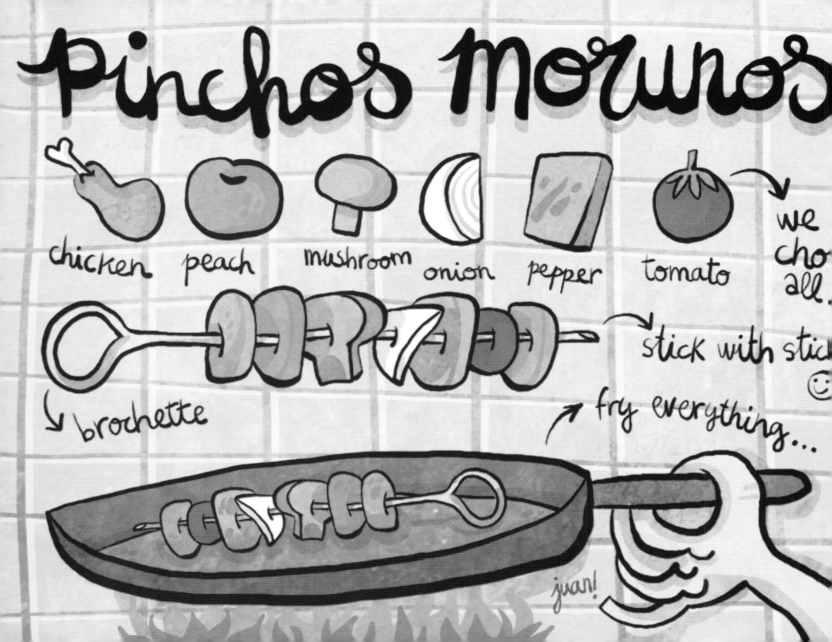

Firebomb

FEEDS 2-4 ☺

GREAT WITH POTATOES

PLACE IN FRYING PAN:
- 1/2 LB SLICED BEEF/CHICKEN
- 3 TBS HOT CHUNKY SALSA
- 1/4 SLICED ONION
- 1 SLICED RED BELL PEPPER
- 1 DICED SERRANO PEPPER
- COOK 10 MIN ON MEDIUM, STIR OFTEN
- FRESH GREEN BEANS
- PINCH OF BLACK PEPPER
- PINCH RED CHILI PEPPER
- 1/4 CUP PICKAPEPPA SAUCE OR SIMILAR

3

SPAGHETTI

in the days when i was much smaller,
sunday night meant dinner at grandmas.
it was served on her white and blue trimmed china
and had a rich aroma that pranced in the wind
all through Cape St. Claire
and although those dinners only persist in memory
the recipe lives on

1 brown (1 lb.) ground beef
in a pot.
drain grease.

2 stir in:
4 cans of tomato soup
4 cans of water
1 chopped onion
1 clove garlic, chopped
2 teaspoons oregano
1/4 teaspoon crushed red peppers
bring to boil, then simmer for 1 hr.

3 cook spaghetti noodles.
drain and rinse.
serve with sauce.

monSter BangERs & mASh

1.

2.
peel & boil POTaTOES
untiL Soft
& TeNDeR...
...draiN WATeR

3.
add
SeaSoning,
& milk,
& BuTTeR...

mash!

milk

get youR
sausages
sizzling...

pile 'em
4. High for a
MONSTER
meaL!

Polpette
di valente

1 LB ground Beef   1/2 cup of Breadcrumbs
1 LB ground Pork   1 cup grated Locatelli Cheese
1 LB ground Veal   Dash of diced fresh Garlic
9 fresh Eggs   Sprinkle of chopped fresh Basil

Mix all ingredients together. Stick your finger
into mixture and make sure there is a hole when
you remove finger. If not, add more Breadcrumbs.
Form mixture into balls and place on ungreased
cookie sheet. Bake in oven at 325°f, until browned.
Remove from oven and place in spaghetti sauce.
Simmer for 3 hours, serve and ENJOY!

TACOS OLÉ!

CHEESE

ingredients (makes 12 tacos)

12 corn tortillas

1lb. ground turkey

1 cup shredded sharp cheddar cheese

2 cups shredded lettuce

2 tomatoes → diced

Taco Sauce

simple to make and so yummy!

5. mix mashed potatoes and onion and beef in a bowl.

6. make flat oval-shaped patties.

1. peel and chop the potatoes.

4. saute onion and beef in a medium skillet.

Flour

PANKO

7. coat each piece with flour. dip in beaten egg. and coat with panko

boil potatoes until soft. drain and mash potatoes while they're hot.

don't forget the tonkatsu sauce!

8. fry in 350°f oil until brown.

korokke

4 medium potatoes

¼ lb. ground beef

½ onion

1 egg

vegetable oil

OIL

flour

panko

PANKO

salt and pepper

Mama's Pancit Miki

Soak 2 lb of rice noodles in hot water until separated. In a frypan, heat 2 tablespoons of oil and saute 1 chopped onion and 4 chopped garlic cloves. Next brown 1 diced chicken breast and 1 lb of peeled prawns. Pour in 1/4 cup soy sauce and 2 tablespoons of oyster sauce with some fresh chopped veggies and stir until heated through. Drain the noodles and add them to the pan with 1/4 cup chicken stock and cook until done.

SPICY TUNA

INGREDIENTS:

SASHIMI GRADE TUNA
1/4 LB

KEWPIE MAYO*
1/4 CUP

SESAME OIL
2 TABLESPOONS

HOT SAUCE
1-2 TEASPOONS

MASAGO
(SMELT ROE, OPTIONAL)

*REGULAR MAYO CAN BE USED

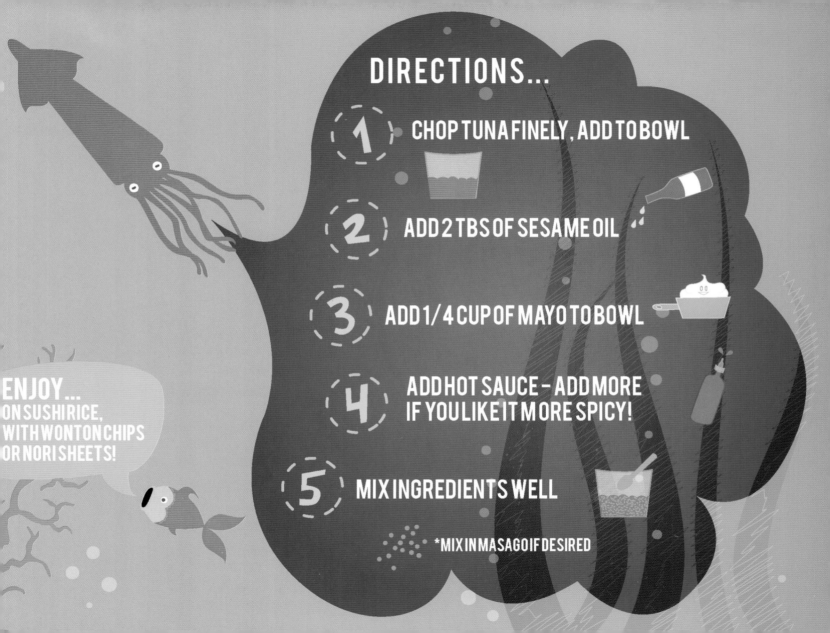

Pan-fried fish with Lemon Caper Sauce

1 lb fish fillets
salt and pepper
4 tbs olive oil
4 tbs butter
1 tbs capers
juice of 1 lemon
1 tsp parsley

season fish with salt
and pepper
heat oil in pan over
medium heat
add fish and cook on
one side until brown
flip over once and
brown on other side
meanwhile heat 1 tbs
of butter in small
saucepan
add lemon juice
parsley and capers
simmer then remove
from heat
add remaining butter
and swirl around until
it is melted
serve fish with butter
sauce drizzled over

Chile & Lime Sea Br

Ingredients

4 Seabream fillets

2 tbsp vegetable oil

5 tbsp soy sauce

2 tbsp brown sugar

2 tbsp cornflour

Method

- Dust seabream in cornflour

- Heat oil in large pan, add seabream and cook for 2-3 minutes on each side. Transfer to a plate and keep warm.

- To the pan add finely sliced garlic, grated ginger and sliced spring onions, fry for 1 minute.

- Add brown sugar, juice of 1 lime and soy sauce, simmer for 1 minute

- Spoon sauce over seabream and scatter thai basil, finely sliced chiles. serve with rice and lime wedges.

6 spring onions

3 garlic cloves

2 chiles, 1 red, 1 green

medium piece of ginger

rice

thai basil

2 limes

MOULES FRITES

24 mussels
1 egg, beaten
4 oz. butter
2 oz. breadcrumbs
1 lemon

Clean the mussels.
Put into a saucepan, on a high heat, with a lid on.
When all the shell's are open, extract the mussel meat and pat dry
on kitchen paper.
Dispose of any mussels that don't open.
Dip each mussel into the beaten egg and then into the breadcrumbs.
Put the butter into a large shallow pan, melt on a medium heat
and add the mussels.
Cook until golden brown.
Serve with cut slices of lemon, with some of the juice squeezed over.

EMPANADA

half *roasted* and peeled red pepper...

half zucchinni...

and half green chile ♡

3.

2.

one onion...

1.

4. two tuna cans ♡

5. spoon some filling in the

a bunch of soaked nori flakes

8-oz tomato sauce

6.

spread

chop → sauté

all chopped

STEP 2

salt

ground black pepper

Provencal herbs

400°F

OVEN 200°

BUTTER

OIL

10 MINS

(ZEST & JUICE)

(HARD BOILED, SLICED)

CAPERS

RICE
(COOKED)

MIX

SALMON

PASTRY

10 in.

FLOUR

12 in.

+

PAN MIX

OVEN
BAKE
35-40 MIN
400°F

333

METHOD

PIE

Grilled Pacific Saury

1. Lightly salt the fish, and grill whole, with head
2. Serve grilled saury with grated daikon radish a
3. To eat, squeeze sudachi over fish. Eat bites of fi
4. Leave bones and guts.

it's never too late to...

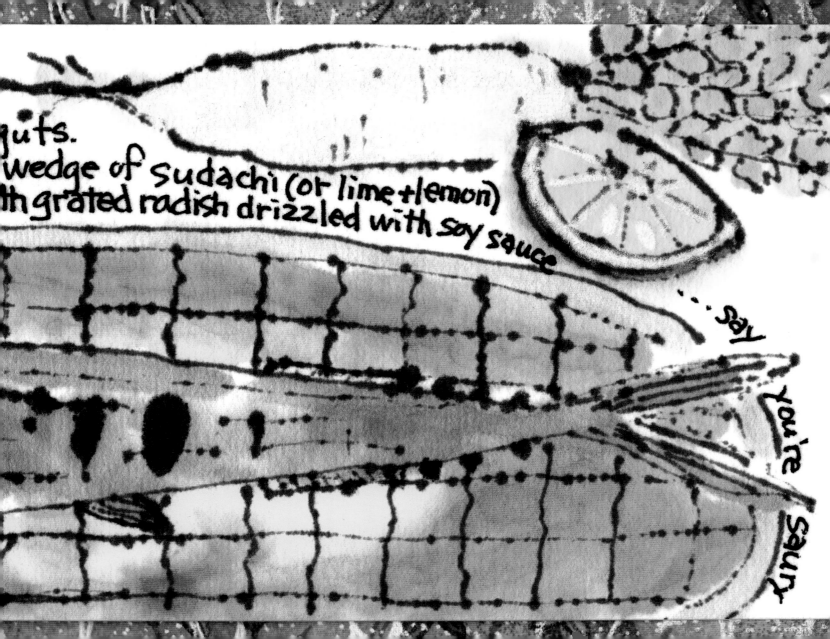

guts.
wedge of sudachi (or lime + lemon)
th grated radish drizzled with soy sauce

...say
you're
saury

CURRY CABBAGE

CHOP

CARROTS MAKE IT LOOK PRETTY!

SLICE

AUBERGINE CAVIAR

2

mic
800
10 m

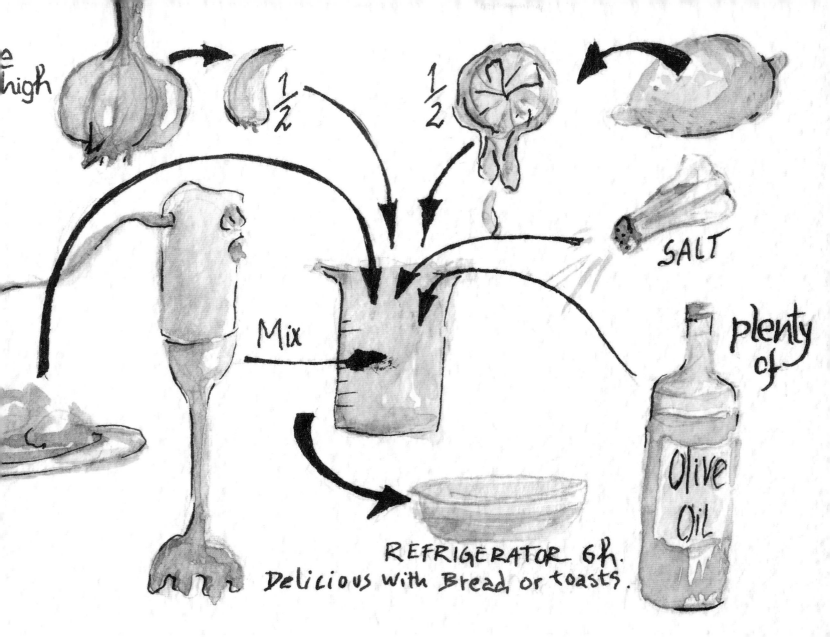

$\frac{1}{2}$

$\frac{1}{2}$

SALT

Mix

plenty of

Olive Oil

REFRIGERATOR 6h.
Delicious with Bread or toasts.

Low Country Geechee Girl's Red Rice

Best made while listening to
Charlie Parker or Retha's "Rock Steady Baby"
In a large pot add 1 TBS of olive oil.
Cut up sausage of your choice.
(Southern brand or whatever floats your boat)
While sausage is browning, cut up 1 sweet yellow onion,
1 green pepper and 2 cloves garlic. Add to sausage and stir.
Cook til meat is nice and brown and veggies are translucent.
Add 1 16 oz. can of tomato sauce and 1/2 can of water.
Add adobo seasoning and salt and pepper to taste.
Let simmer for 10-20 minutes. Add 1 1/2 tsp. of sugar.
Stir in 2 cups of long grain white rice and cook til
all liquid is absorbed and rice is tender.
Serve with cornbread and sweet tea!

Want to kick it up a notch? Add some fresh shrimp
and corn. And red pepper flakes for an extra kick!

GARLIC MASHED POTATOES
10 POTATOES, 8 GARLIC CLOVES, 8 OUNCES SOUR CREAM
8 OUNCES CREAM CHEESE, 4 OUNCES BUTTER

POTATOES MULTILEVEL

5 POTATOES

1/3 lb. HAM

1/2 cup GRATED PARMESAN CHEESE

BLACK PEPPER

6 1/2 oz. SCAMORZA CHEESE

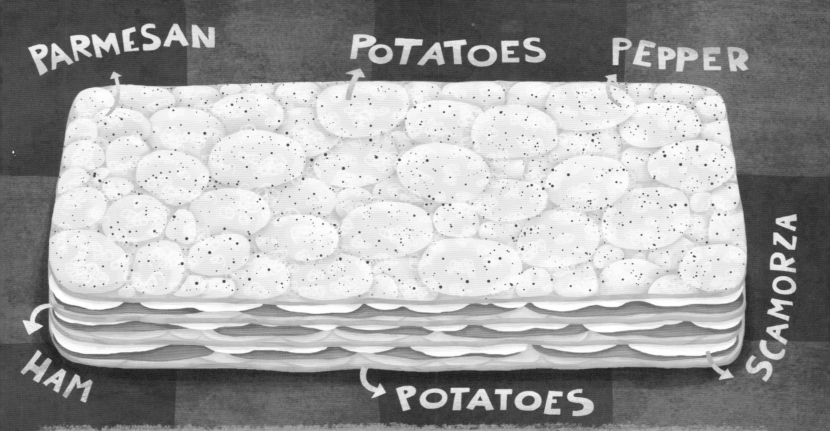

PARMESAN

POTATOES

PEPPER

SCAMORZA

HAM

POTATOES

Thinly slice potatoes, ham and scamorza cheese.
Cover a baking pan with parchment paper.
Prepare a first layer with potatoes and place slices of ham
and scamorza on top. Leave some space between each slice.
Repeat twice and finish with a last layer of potatoes,
grated parmesan cheese and a sprinkle of black pepper.
Bake in preheated 425°F oven for about 1 hour.

thingummyjig

chop it (the beetroot) into little bits making certain to eat a few bits as you go

(the recipe <u>will</u> <u>not</u> work if you don't do this)

add some nice creamy natural yogurt & some salt & pepper & mix it together. It will be this colour (ish)

yumtious!

(try it on a cracker)

"OH MY HECK! SOMEBODY DIED!"

Mormon Funeral Potatoes

10 medium potatoes

1/2 cup plus 2 tablespoons melted butter

2 cans condensed cream of mushroom

or cream of chicken soup

1 1/2 cups grated cheddar cheese

2 cups crushed cornflakes

2 cups sour cream

1/2 finely diced onion

Peel and boil potatoes until just tender.
In a bowl, combine soup, 1/2 cup melted butter,
sour cream, onions and cheese.
Grate the potatoes and stir into the bowl.
Pour mixture into a greased 9" x 13" pan.
Add salt and pepper to taste.
Combine cornflakes with 2 tablespoons
melted butter and sprinkle over pan.
Bake at 350°f for 30-45 minutes
until hot and bubbly.

"LADAWN! LAVAR!
NEPHI! BRIGHAM!

WHICH ONE OF YOU
KIDS HID THE FLIPPIN'
POTATO PEELER?!"

coconut macaroons

1 ⅓ cup sweet flaked coconut
½ cup sugar
2 tablespoons flour
⅛ teaspoon salt
2 egg whites
½ teaspoon vanilla

Combine all ingredients. Stir well.
Drop rounded teaspoonfuls on to greased cookie sheet.
Bake at 325°f for 18-20 minutes until golden-tipped.
Cool on rack. Makes 12.

Brownies

by Echo

4 tbsp Cocoa

2 eggs

½ cup of Margarine

½ tsp Vanilla

1 Cup Brown sugar

BOWL 1

Mix together until smooth

Chocolate CRÊPE

OOOh
LA
LA

1 cup flour
½ cup milk
½ cup water
2 Tbsp Butter
2 eggs
A Bit of salt
A Chocolate Bar
(melted)

Mix up ingredients
Heat Buttered pan on medium
Pour batter into Frying pan
Flip When bottom is light brown color
Pour/Spoon melted Chocolate onto ½ side of Crêpe, flip in half
Serve ★ Top with fruit or Whipped Cream

Lk

flip ½

NUM
NUM
NUM

NUM
NUM
NUM

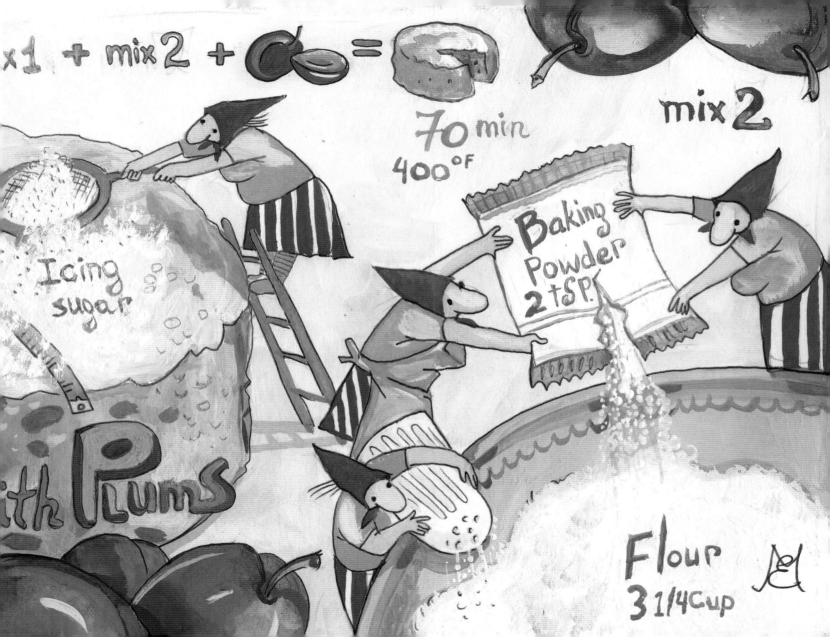

BORUTA
&
Gourmandine
PRESENT:

"Alors, Gourmandine, qu'allons-nous préparer aujourd'hui?"

BORUTA's
CHEESECAKE
* * *

INGREDIENTS:
24 oz. soft fresh cheese,
3 eggs,
3/4 cup sugar,
1 stick of butter,
1 tsp. baking powder,
3 tbsp. semolina,
1 pack of vanilla pudding powder,
raisins, petit-beurre biscuits

Cover the bottom of your baking form with petit-beurre biscuits.

Separate the egg whites from the yolks.

Mix sugar, butter and yolks.

Gradually add cheese, semolina, baking powder, pudding powder and a pinch of salt.

Add raisins to the mixture.

Beat stiffly egg whites and add slowly to the mixture.

Pour the mixture into the form.

Bake at 400°f for about an hour.

KEKSLOLLIS

biscuitlollies

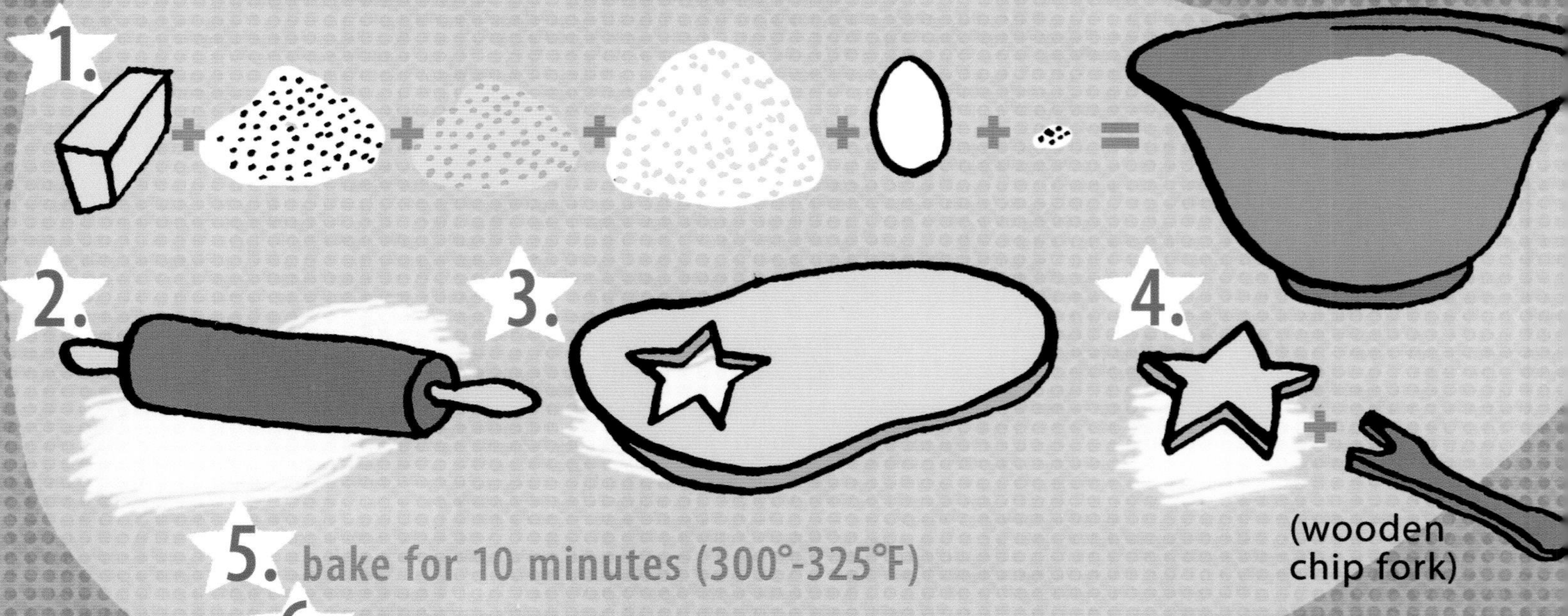

1. ▮ + ◭ + ◭ + ◭ + ⬭ + ∴ = 🥣

2. 🧹(rolling pin)

3. ⬭ with ★ cutout

4. ★ + 🍴 (wooden chip fork)

5. bake for 10 minutes (300°-325°F)

6. cool on the baking tray and decorate with icing and food colouring

6 1/2 tablespoons butter
6 tablespoons sugar
3/4 cup ground almonds
1 1/8 cup flour
1 egg
pinch of salt

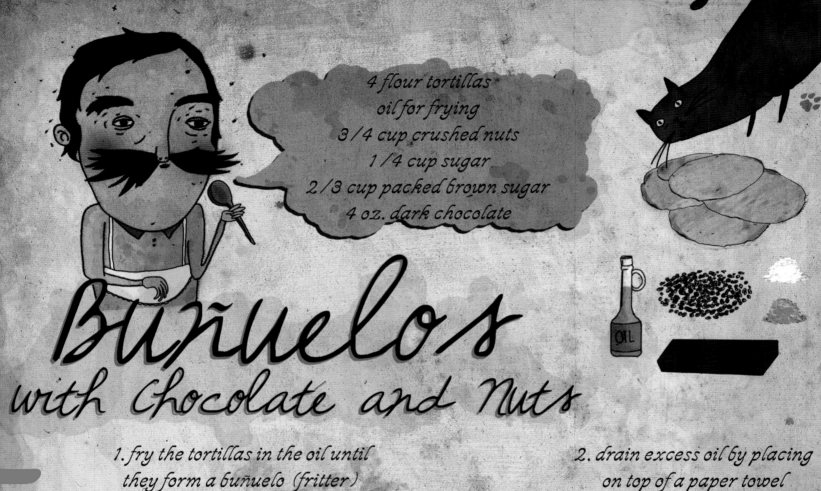

4 flour tortillas
oil for frying
3/4 cup crushed nuts
1/4 cup sugar
2/3 cup packed brown sugar
4 oz. dark chocolate

Buñuelos
with Chocolate and Nuts

1. fry the tortillas in the oil until they form a buñuelo (fritter)

2. drain excess oil by placing on top of a paper towel

MONKEY BANANA CREAM!

INGREDIENTS FOR 4 PEOPLE

- 3 BANANAS
- 1/2 LEMON
- 8 TABLESPOONS GREEK NATURAL YOGURT
- 6 TABLESPOONS MASCARPONE CHEESE
- 4 TEASPOONS HONEY
- 6 WALNUTS

1. PEEL AND CHOP THE BANANAS, PUT THEM IN A BOWL AND MASH THEM. ADD LEMON JUICE AND MIX.

2. ADD THE YOGURT, MASCARPONE AND HONEY. MIX WELL.

3. CHOP WALNUTS INTO SMALL PIECES.

4. SERVE IN INDIVIDUAL BOWLS AND SPRINKLE WITH WALNUTS. YOU CAN ADD CINNAMON POWDER, CHOCOLATE SHAVINGS OR WHATEVER YOUR IMAGINATION SAYS. MONKEY LIKES EVERYTHING AS LONG AS IT'S BANANAS!

NATURAL YOGURT

MASCARPONE

HONEY

you will need:

- 1 3/4 cups Self Rising flour
- 1/2 tsp baking powder
- 1 Cup Superfine Sugar
- 1/4 Cup Brown Sugar
- 1 Cup Butter, plus extra for greasing
- 4 Eggs
- 2/3 Cup Natural yogurt
- 1 tsp Vanilla extract
- 1 large tin pineapple rings
- A handful raisins

1 Heat your oven to 350°F. Butter your cake tin and scatter lots of brown sugar all over. Arrange the pineapple and raisins in a pretty pattern.

2 Beat together the sugar and butter, then mix in the vanilla, yogurt and eggs. Now gently mix in the flour and baking powder.

3 Now spoon the cake mixtu[re] over the pineapple then bake for 50 min's or until skewer comes out clean.

Cool a little, then run a kni[fe] around the edge and turn out onto a board.

AFRICAN Lemon Cookies

INGREDIENTS:

For the dough

2.5 cups flour

.5 cup of butter

.5 cup sugar

2 eggs

1 Tbsp baking powder

To decorate

1 2/3 cup icing sugar
juice of one lemon
zest of one lemon,
washed and grated

Sift the flour with baking powder, make the fountain and add the sugar, softened butter and cut into small pieces and eggs.
Mix thoroughly and quickly, put to rest in refrigerator for 30 minutes, wrapped with plastic wrap.

With a rolling pin, roll out the pastry dough to about half an inch thick and cut cookies using SPECIAL MOLDS. Line a pan with a sheet of baking paper, place the cookies and bake in preheated oven (350 degrees) for about 10 minutes.

Mix icing sugar with the juice and lemon zest until to get a frosting.
Put the frosting on cookies with a spoon.

SLURP!!

Zesty LEMON
CHEESECAKE
It'll make your tastebuds go zing!

Ingredients:

FOR THE CRUST—

6 1/2 oz Tennis Biscuits or any other coconut digestive biscuits
1/2 Cup unsalted butter
1 Tbs. White sugar

FOR THE FILLING—

2 Cups full-fat small curd cottage cheese
1/2 Cup heavy cream
3 Free Range eggs
2/3 Cup Sugar
1 Tsp Vanilla Extract
Juice of 1/2 lemon
2 Tbs Lemon Curd

FOR THE TOPPING—

Zest of 1 lemon

When life hands you lemons—
Make this Zesty Cheesecake.

Putting it All Together:

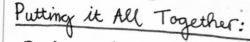

- Preheat the oven to 350°F
- Mix crushed biscuits with melted butter and sugar. Press crust into a baking dish or a spring form pan.
- Mix together all the filling ingredients and pour into crust.
- Bake cheesecake for 15 min.

- Reduce heat to 300°F.
- Bake cheesecake for another 20min
- Let cake cool with oven door open.

- Scatter with lemon zest and serve sliced at room temperature

COOK'S NOTE

IF YOU CAN WAIT, THIS CAKE TASTES BETTER WHEN RESTED FOR ONE DAY.

* PREPARE YOURSELF FOR LOTS OF COMPLIMENTS! *

Mom-Mom's Perfect Peach Cake

Make the RICH SWEET DOUGH first!

Scald the milk to an almost BOIL

Stir! in sugar, salt, & butter

Cool to Luke Warm

in a separate BOWL, add Warm Water

then...

SPRINKLE in the YEAST & stir! until dissolved

Mix in Milk, EGG & half of the FLOUR

BEAT smooth while adding the rest of the FLOUR

3/4 cup of Milk

Scalded

SUGAR 1/2 cup

2 tsp. SALT

FLOUR

1

cover tightly with wax paper

Refrigerate ✶✶ at least 2 hours...

DOUGH MAYBE KEPT REFRIGERATED FOR UP TO 3 DAYS

Cut off DOUGH desired, depending on PAN SIZE

Let raise until ① Double Bulk in greased Pan

Cut & Slice Fresh Peaches

next...

Mix some cinnamon & sugar after brushing + melted BUTTER over DOUGH, ARRANGE Peaches in a spiral pattern & Dust with cinnamon sugar mixture

BAKE at 375°F for 25 minutes

after baking sprinkle heavily with confectioners SUGAR

unsifted FLOUR

½ cup of WARM WATER

cakes YEAST 2

1 EGG

4 cups

...TER

Red Velvet Cookies

Melt three ounces unsweetend baking chocolate with one half cup of butter. In a large mixing bowl, beat the mixture with two-thirds of a cup of brown sugar and one-third of a cup of white sugar.
Beat in one egg and one egg yolk.
Beat in three quarters of a cup of sour cream until lightly fluffy.
Add a teaspoon of dry red food coloring.

Sour Cream

2/3

1/3

one teaspoon
Salt

Baking Soda
one teaspoon

A CUP OF FLOUR

Combine dry ingredients, one cup of flour, and one teaspoon each of baking soda and salt. Sift slowly over the butter/sugar/chocolate mix. Beat until combined, but do not over beat.

CLASSIC Tiramisu

INGREDIENTS

6 egg yolks
1 1/4 cups white sugar
1 1/4 cups mascarpone cheese
1 3/4 cups heavy whipping cream
2 (12 ounce) packages ladyfingers
1/3 cup coffee flavored liqueur

1 tsp unsweetened cocoa powder
1 ounce square semisweet chocolate

DIRECTIONS

1 Combine sugar and egg yolks in the top of a double boiler, over boiling water.

Reduce heat to low, and cook for about 10 minutes, stirring constantly.

Remove from heat and whip yolks until thick and lemon colored.

Add mascarpone cheese to whipped yolks. Beat until combined.

2 In a separate bowl, whip cream to stiff peaks.

Gently fold the whipped cream into the yolk mixture.

Set aside.

3 Split the lady fingers in half, lining the bottom and sides of a large glass bowl with the split ladyfingers.

Brush with coffee liqueur.

Spoon half of the cream filling over the lady fingers.

Repeat ladyfingers, coffee liqueur and filling layers.

Garnish with cocoa and chocolate curls.

Refrigerate several hours or overnight.

4 To make the chocolate curls, run a vegetable peeler down the edge of a chocolate bar.

MADELEINES

- 2 EGGS
- 3/4 CUP SUGAR
- 1 CUP FLOUR
- 1/2 CUP MELTED BUTTER

HEAT OVEN TO 400°F. GREASE A 12-HOLE MADELEINE PAN. WHISK EGGS + SUGAR TOGETHER UNTIL THICK + PALE. FOLD IN FLOUR THEN BUTTER. PUT 2 TSP OF MIXTURE INTO EACH MADELEINE MOLD. BAKE FOR 6 MINUTES.   MAKES 24.

SIMPLE CAKE

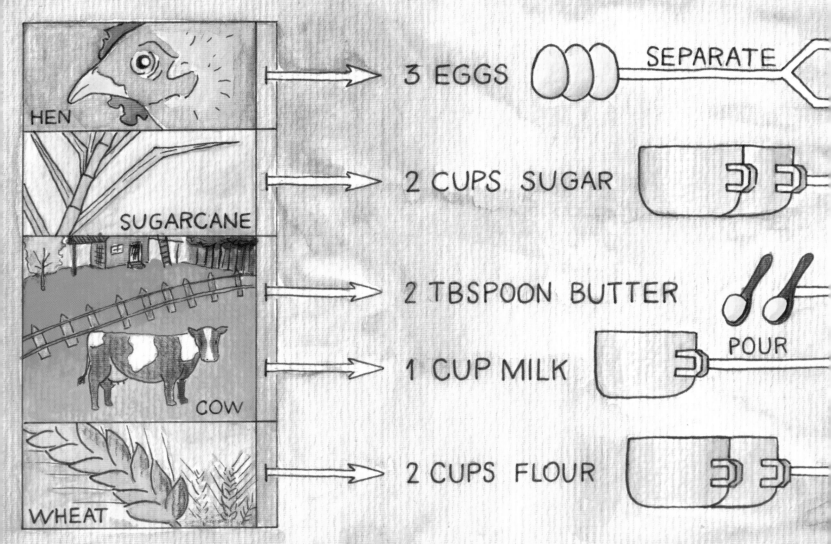

HEN → 3 EGGS — SEPARATE

SUGARCANE → 2 CUPS SUGAR

→ 2 TBSPOON BUTTER

COW → 1 CUP MILK — POUR

WHEAT → 2 CUPS FLOUR

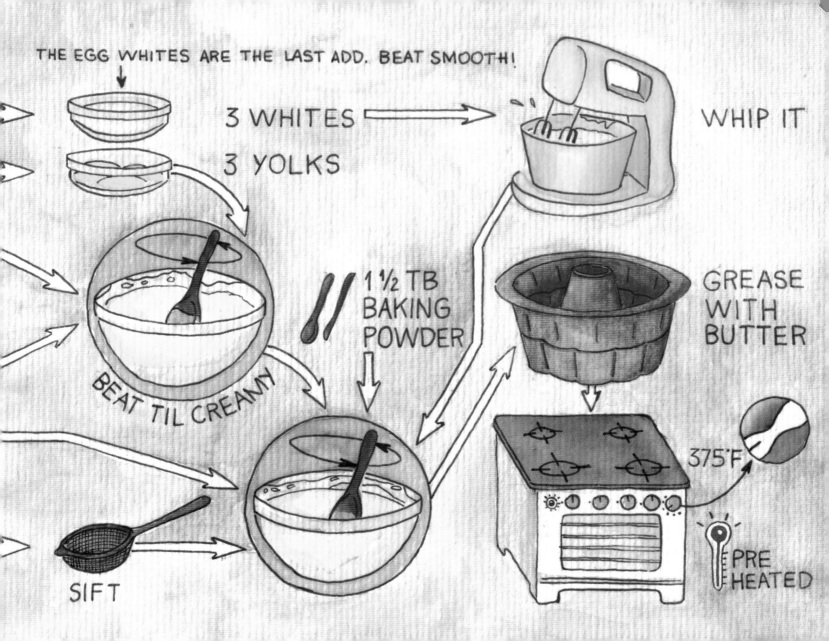

classic CUPCAKES

ingredients

* 2 cups self-raising flour
* 3/4 cup caster sugar
* 3/4 cup milk
* 9 tbs butter, melted, cooled
* 2 eggs - beaten
* 1 teaspoon - vanilla essence
* Sprinkles & lollies!

ICING

* 1 1/2 CUPS ICING SUGAR
* food colouring
* 1-1 1/2 tablespoons water

* STEP 1 *

Preheat oven to 400°f
Grease up muffin tray
Combine flour + Caster Sugar in a bowl
& make a well in the centre

* STEP 2 *

Add milk, butter + eggs & vanilla
To flour mix
using a large wooden spoon
Stir gently to combine

* STEP 3 *

Spoon mixture into prepared muffin pan
Bake for 12-15 minutes

Stand in pan for 5 minutes before
transfering onto wire rack

* STEP 4 * [MAKING ICING]

Sift icing Sugar into bowl
Add food colouring & water
Stir until smooth & well combined
Spoon over cupcakes
Decorate with sprinkles + lollies

YUM
YUM
YUM

Chef Kitty's Top Secret
Chocolate Chip Cookies

Ingredients:

3/4 cup packed
brown sugar

2 1/4 cups of
all-purpose flour

1 tsp vanilla
extract

1 tsp baking soda

1 tsp salt

1 cup butter,
softened

3/4 cup
granulated
sugar

2 Large Eggs

12 oz. Semi-sweet
chocolate chips

YUM!

2 COMBINE flour, baking soda and salt in small bowl.

PREHEAT oven to 375 degrees F.

3 Beat butter, granulated sugar, brown sugar and vanilla extract in large mixer bowl until creamy.

4 Add eggs one at a time, beating well after each addition. Gradually beat in flour mixture.

5 Stir in chocolate chips.

6 Scoop rounded tablespoon of mixture on an ungreased baking sheet.

7 BAKE for 9 to 11 minutes or until golden brown.

8 Transfer to wire rack to cool.

we're the best!

Serve with a tall glass of milk!

Enjoy!

-Chef Kitty

©Jannie Ho

gueffus

4 cups of ground almonds
2 cups of sugar
1–2 cups sambuca
1 strip lemon zest
3/4 cup plus 3 tablespoons of water
more sugar

Make a syrup with the sugar and
the water and add the ground
almonds, 1 or 2 glasses of sambuca
and the lemon zest.
Simmer a few minutes, turn off
and let it cool completely.
Bathe your hands in sambuca and
form little balls, then pass
them in a bowl with sugar.
Cut coloured tissue paper for food
into rectangles (you can also cut
the sides into strips) and wrap each
ball into them.

(my grandmas used to make them...)

MIX

ROLL

1 1/8 cup Flour

2 Egg Yolks

1/3 cup Corn Starch

1/3 cup Sugar

6 1/2 tbsp Butter

1 tsp Baking Powder

into one or more logs

some special ingredient! like

choc chips, coffee powder, lemon zest, cocoa, toasted hazelnut

COOKIES

CHILL

Freezer
30 min

or

Fridge
1 hour

CUT

3/8 inch thick
cookies

tip!
combine 2
flavours

BAKE

at 325° in a CONVECTION oven
or 350° in a NORMAL one

15 for min

chocolate and orange zest, cinnamon, walnuts and brown sugar.

Soufflé au fromage

Quark Soufflé

1 cup Quark

3 large eggs

3 tablespoons flour

1/8 tablespoons salt

1 teaspoon vanilla extract

1/8 tsp. Cream of tartar

1/4 cup sugar

In a medium bowl, whisk together the Quark, egg yolks, flour, salt, and vanilla. In a large bowl of a stand mixer beat the egg whites with cream of tartar until soft peaks. Gradually add sugar, continuing to beat, until the whites are 'stiff' but not dry. Scrape the cheese mixture onto the egg whites and fold together gently. Divide the batter among the ramekins and sprinkle top of each with sugar. Bake until soufflés are puffed and golden brown.

Make a pot
of coffee

Pour it into an
ice cube tray
freeze overnight

lend with
ugar and
milk

Serve with
chocolate on
bottom and
condensed milk
on top.

White chocolate and Spices hot drink

2 cups Whole Milk
2 anise stars
2 Cinnamon Sticks
1/2 Split Vanilla bean
1 White chocolate bar (3.5 oz)
a pinch of salt

Warm in pot : Milk, Cinnamon Sticks, Vanilla, Salt, Mix together and Heat

Strain in Strainer over bowl, and Mix With White chocolate Until the White chocolate Melts

Pour into cups, and decorate With anise & Cinnamon Sticks !

DRINK WHILE WARM.

by Tatiana DOROKHINA

Hong Kong Style Super Lemon iced Tea

we use **Black Tea**, in tea bags. but you can also use tea leaves if you prefer that. make yourself a cup of tea!! Simple as that, but we're not just making any ordinary cup o' tea. So after you make that Hot cup of tea, while it's Still hot, add 1 teaspoon of sugar. You can always add more sugar. but that just isn't Hong Kong Style iced tea anymore. Adding syrup instead of sugar would be great too!

teabags

tea

sugar
1 tsp

since i 1st laid my taste buds on that iced tea . . . . . .

lemons

lemon rind
lemon zest

grater

ice

drink & enjoy

We simply must add ice! it wouldn't <u>be</u> iced tea without <u>ICE</u>. Next is transferring the tea in a nice clear tall glass. Finally we add 2-3 slices of lemon or if you want it to be more "lemony", just use the skin of the lemon, and using a grater, grate the skin and VOILA! You have lemon zest. Add that to the drink and presto! You have now made Love. 香港檸檬茶!! ♥

best enjoyed during a hot summer afternoon. ☀
or have an "iced" tea party !!

...i instantly fell in Love with it... ♥ Enjoy!!

fresh lemonade

lemons

sugar

ice cubes

water

Mango Lassi

- 4 large ice cubes
  (vary quantity depending
  on desired consistency)

- 1 cup plain low-fat yogurt
  (can use vanilla yogurt instead
  for added flavor)

- 1 medium mango,
  peeled and cubed

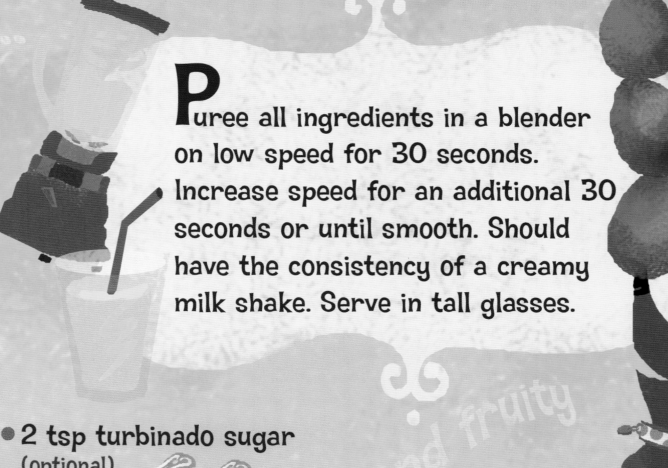

Puree all ingredients in a blender on low speed for 30 seconds. Increase speed for an additional 30 seconds or until smooth. Should have the consistency of a creamy milk shake. Serve in tall glasses.

- 2 tsp turbinado sugar
(optional)

cold and fruity

joy steuerwald

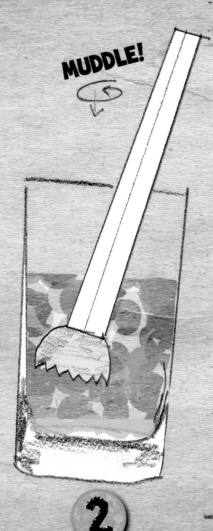

ICE

1 OZ. RUM

3 OZ.
CLUB SODA

MINT TO GARNISH

3

ENJOY!

PIMM'S
N°1

Classic Pimms:

Ice

1 measure
    Pimms Nº1

3 measures
    Ginger Ale

1 slice lemon

1 slice
    Cucumber

1 slice apple

Fresh Mint

1 cup flour
1 cup water
1/2 cup salt
1 tablespoon oil
2 teaspoons cream of tartar
10–15 drops of food coloring

HOMEMADE  *play dough*

little hands measure + stir all the ingredients in a sauce pan. **adult hands** cook mixture at **medium** heat until it *just starts to cook,* **stirring continuously!** dough is done when it looks like sticky play–dough. **dump mixture onto a lightly floured** cutting board until cool enough to handle. knead until smooth. **PLAY** [store in airtight container] **PLAY MORE,** repeat.

INDEX OF ARTISTS
(in order of appearance)

→

MORI San Diego, CA
rahmori.com

ANNA AFONINA Bryansk, Russia
annscreativeblog.blogspot.com

NAZANIN KANI Atlanta, GA

ROBERTA & DEBORA BLONKOWSKI Curitiba, Brazil

ZIUBAK Poznan, Poland
wczyk.blogspot.com

KIM FLEMING Melbourne, Australia
kimflemingillustration.com

AMANDA KASTNER Bemidji, MN
amandakastner.com

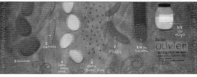

DINARA MIRTALIPOVA Tashkent, Uzbekistan
mirdinara.blogspot.com

GADE Ludwigsburg, Germany
ade.com

ESTHER LOOPSTRA Seattle, WA
estherloopstra.com

JORDI FARRÉS TAÑA Vic (Barcelona), Spain
k-s-x.blogspot.com

KAMINI RAGHAVAN Hyderabad, India
saffronandsilk.blogspot.com

EILLY Medina, OH

ALEXANDRE ALDEGUER Elx, Spain
mondongofanzine.blogspot.com

BETSY SNYDER Independence, OH
betsysnyder.com

RACHEL LEWIS London, UK
rachelsayshello.com

A. BELL Minneapolis, MN
bell.com

LISA GRAVES Medway, MA
lisagravesdesign.net

PAULA PERTILE CA
paulapertile.com

NAOMI BARDOFF Oakland, CA
naomibardoff.com

OLLAK Providence, RI
ks.com

STEFANIE HESS Bern, Switzerland
kwerbeet.ch

HEATH KILLEN Newcastle, Australia
madebyhk.com

DANIEL JANSSON Umeå, Sweden
inspiram.se

IRENA INUMARU London, UK
irena-inumaru.com

JUAN DÍAZ-FAES DÍAZ Oviedo, Spain
juandiazfaes.blogspot.com

PETER BREESE Ann Arbor, MI
peterbreese.com

SARAH STRAUB Annapolis, MD
sarahstraub.com

SARAH WARD Sheffield, UK
gingerbred.co.uk

KEVIN VALENTE Baltimore, MD
kevinrileyvalente.blogspot.com

SHARON MANN Las Vegas, NV
sharonmanndesigns.com

KATHLEEN MARCOTTE Elmhurst, IL
kathleenmarcotte.com

KAILI ITTENSOHN Brisbane, Australia
kailiittensohn.com

ILARIA FALORSI Firenze, Italy
ilariafalorsi.com

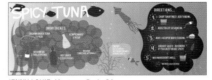

JENNY LOUIE Monterey Park, CA
jennylouie.com

PAT GARMHAUSEN Cleveland Heights, OH
giardino.etsy.com

JOHNATHAN HAWKER Loughborough, Leicestershire, UK
anotherhp.wordpress.com

HANNAH CLARK Kent, UK
hannahclarkillustration.com

CAILIN NEALON Baltimore, MD
cailinart.tumblr.com

ALYA MARK Madrid, Spain
cartooncooking.blogspot.com

ALICE DANSEY-WRIGHT Glasgow, Scotland
dwdsketchbook.blogspot.com

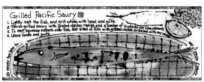

DEBORAH DAVIDSON (DOSANKODEBBIE) Sapporo, Japan
etegamibydosankodebbie.blogspot.com

NATE PADAVICK North Adams, MA
studiosss.com

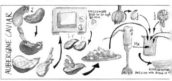

SOFIA MATALONGA JORGE Lisbon, Portugal
aranhalinhas.blogspot.com

JAMES GULLIVER HANCOCK Brooklyn, NY
jamesgulliverhancock.com

VANESSA BRANTLEY-NEWTON East Orange, NJ
oohlaladesignstudio.blogspot.com

MEG GUERIN Seattle, WA
megwee.com

SILVIA SPONZA Milano, Italy
silviasponza.ultra-book.com

ROTHWELL Nottingham, UK
hwell.co.uk

JANE DIXON St. Charles, IL
janedixon.com

JOHANNA BAILEY Barcelona, Spain
barcelonabites.com

CÉLESTE GAGNON Markham, Ontario, Canada
doodlesscribbles.blogspot.com

MCCANE Wilmington, DE
cane.com

EKATERINA MURATOVA Moscow, Russia
illustrators.ru/user/6845/portfolio

KAJETANA FIDLER Lausanne, Switzerland
cayetanca.blogspot.com

SILKE SCHMIDT Berlin, Germany
silkeundich.de

W Brooklyn, NY
om

TANIA BASURTO Hermosillo, México
taniabasurto.carbonmade.com

DANIELA GARRETON Santiago, Chile
dagarreton.tumblr.com

CLAIRE B. MURRAY Glasgow, Scotland
clairemurray.co.uk

BOSSÚ Turin, Italy
ossu.carbonmade.com

TANYA TURIPAMWE STROH Windhoek, Namibia
tanyaturi.blogspot.com

KRISTIN NOHE Bel Air, MD
kristinnohe.com

JENNIFER WEBER New York City, NY
runliljared.com

AYES Ann Arbor, MI
andpolkadots.com

JESSICA BARNES Brisbane, Australia
drgateau.com

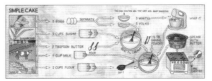
NAIARA TALAMINI & CAULI TOMAZ Curitiba, Brazil

HORACIO GUZMÁN AGUIRRE Tokyo, Japan
chicolelediary.blogspot.com

IES TURNBULL Sydney, Australia
esturnbull.com

JANNIE HO Ann Arbor, MI
chickengirldesign.com

PAOLO BAKIS MURGIA Cagliari, Sardinia
flavors.me/bakis

PIETRO DUCHI Cremona, Italy
eggpete.tumblr.com

META WRABER Ljubljana, Slovenia
metamundus.blogspot.com

EULALIA MEJÍA Medellín, Colombia
happychinchilla.net

OR LIVNEH Tel Aviv, Israel
orlivneh.blogspot.com

TATIANA DOROKHINA Nizhny Novgorod, Russia
dorokhina.blogspot.com

AUDZ ANG Manila, Philippines
mylifeisadoodle.blogspot.com

VALENTINA RAMOS Miami, FL
valentinadesign.com

ABZ HAKIM Toronto, Canada
abzhakim.com

JOY STEUERWALD Fremont, CA
joystewy.com

JAMES ORNDORF Skull Valley, AZ
roughshelter.com

REBECCA BRADLEY Baltimore, MD
lillarogers.com

DIANA HEOM San Francisco, CA
dianaheom.com

MARTHA CLARK-PLANK Cleveland, OH
squarepegsymposium.blogspot.com

THEY DRAW & COOK

STUDIO SSS, LLC
Bossy Brother Nate Padavick
Silly Sister Salli Swindell
studiosss.com

First printed in 2011
10 9 8 7 6 5 4 3 2 1

Library of Congress Control Number:
2011920829

ISBN 13: 978-1-61628-138-0
ISBN 10: 1-61628-138-3

weldon**owen**

415 Jackson Street, Suite 200
San Francisco, CA 94111
wopublishing.com

WELDON OWEN, INC.
CEO and President Terry Newell
VP, Sales and Marketing Amy Kaneko
Director of Finance Mark Perrigo
VP and Publisher Hannah Rahill
Associate Publisher Amy Marr
Editor Julia Humes
Creative Director Emma Boys
Associate Art Director Diana Heom
Production Director Chris Hemesath
Production Manager Michelle Duggan

Printed and bound by 1010 Printing
International Ltd. in China

Weldon Owen is a division of
BONNIER

A VERY SPECIAL THANKS to the artists whose wonderful artwork inspired or contributed to the design of this book: Martha Clark-Plank, Eliza DeVogel, Daniela Garreton, Christina Kent, Eulalia Mejía, Alex Savakis, Sarah Straub, and Meta Wraber.

Artwork by Meta Wraber

A VERY SPECIAL THANKS to the artists whose wonderful artwork inspired or contributed to the design of this book: Martha Clark-Plank, Eliza DeVogel, Daniela Garreton, Christina Kent, Eulalia Mejía, Alex Savakis, Sarah Straub, and Meta Wraber.

Artwork by Meta Wraber

Artwork by Eulalia Mejía